AF428395

AMAZING WONDERS AROUND THE GLOBE!

WONDERS OF THE WORLD
CHILDREN'S REFERENCE BOOKS

In this book, we're going to talk about amazing wonders that exist around the globe. So, let's get right to it!

HERODOTUS

During ancient times, Herodotus, the historian, and Callimachus of Cyrene, the scholar, compiled a list of the "Seven Wonders." Of these classic seven wonders, including the Lighthouse at Alexandria and the Statue of Zeus at Olympia, only one of those wonders is still standing. It is the Great Pyramid of Giza, which was built around 2560 BC.

In the year 2001, a corporation in Switzerland decided to begin a project to select a new group of seven wonders. After reviewing over 200 different monuments, the following ones were selected:

- The Great Wall of China, built in China
- Petra, built in Jordan
- Christ the Redeemer, built in Brazil
- Machu Picchu, built in Peru
- Chichén Itzá, built in Mexico
- The Colosseum, built in Italy
- The Taj Mahal, built in India

RUINS OF OLYMPIA TEMPLE

They also listed the Great Pyramid of Giza as an honorary member of the list.

GREAT PYRAMID OF GIZA

THE GREAT WALL OF CHINA

The Great Wall is a symbol of the country of China. It's actually many different walls as well as fortifications such as watchtowers. The Wall was measured in 2012 by China's Cultural Heritage Administration and was found to be 13,171 miles long, over twice the length that had been previously recorded. Many of the Wall's structures run in parallel lines with each other.

The very first emperor of unified China, Emperor Qin Shi Huang, began the Wall's construction in the 3rd century BC. It was designed to keep nomads, called barbarians, out of the country. It provided more of a psychological barrier than a physical barrier. One of the most complex and extensive manmade constructions ever built, the section that is best known as well as best preserved was built during the Ming dynasty from the year 1368 through the year 1644 AD.

EMPEROR QIN SHI HUANG

Prior to Emperor Qin Shi Huang, the country of China was separated into smaller kingdoms. This period of China's history has been described as the Warring States era. Once Emperor Qin unified the country, he ordered that walls between the

kingdoms come down and that walls started on the country's north border be connected into one wall extending the length of 10,000 li. A "li" is the same as about 1/3 of a mile.

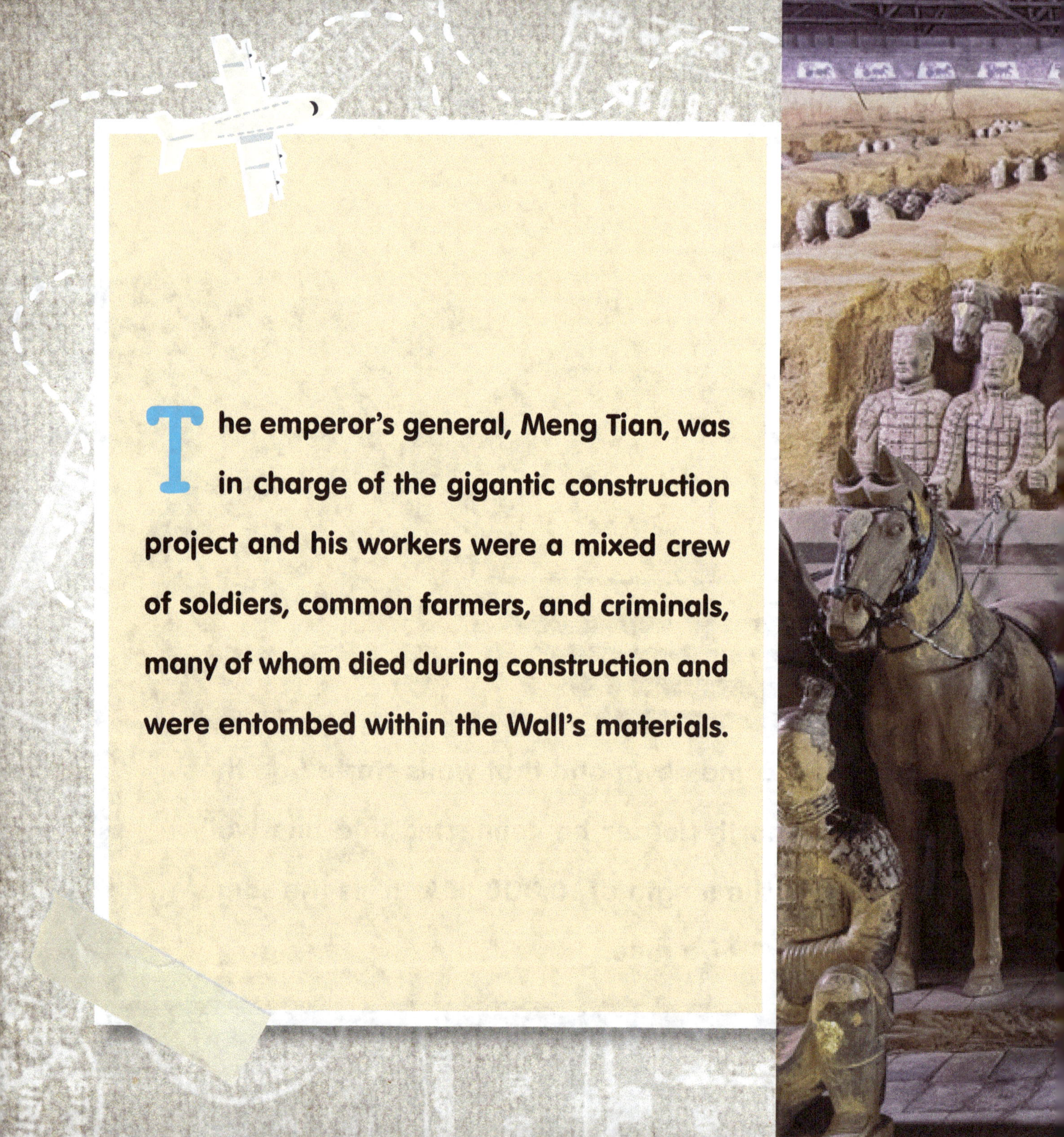

The emperor's general, Meng Tian, was in charge of the gigantic construction project and his workers were a mixed crew of soldiers, common farmers, and criminals, many of whom died during construction and were entombed within the Wall's materials.

TERRACOTTA ARMY

Throughout the centuries, the Wall went into a state of disrepair or was rebuilt or additions were made many times. Most of the Wall that people visit today was constructed during the powerful Ming dynasty. The culture of the country thrived during the reign of the Ming rulers. In addition to the Great Wall, they also took on vast numbers of other types of building projects including construction of complex bridges as well as elaborate temples and pagodas.

PETRA

Petra in Jordan is often described as the "Rose City" due to the color of its towering cliffs of sandstone. The city was carved directly into the rock. In fact, its name comes from the Greek word for "rocks," which is "petros."

ANCIENT TEMPLE IN PETRA

ANCIENT CITY OF PETRA

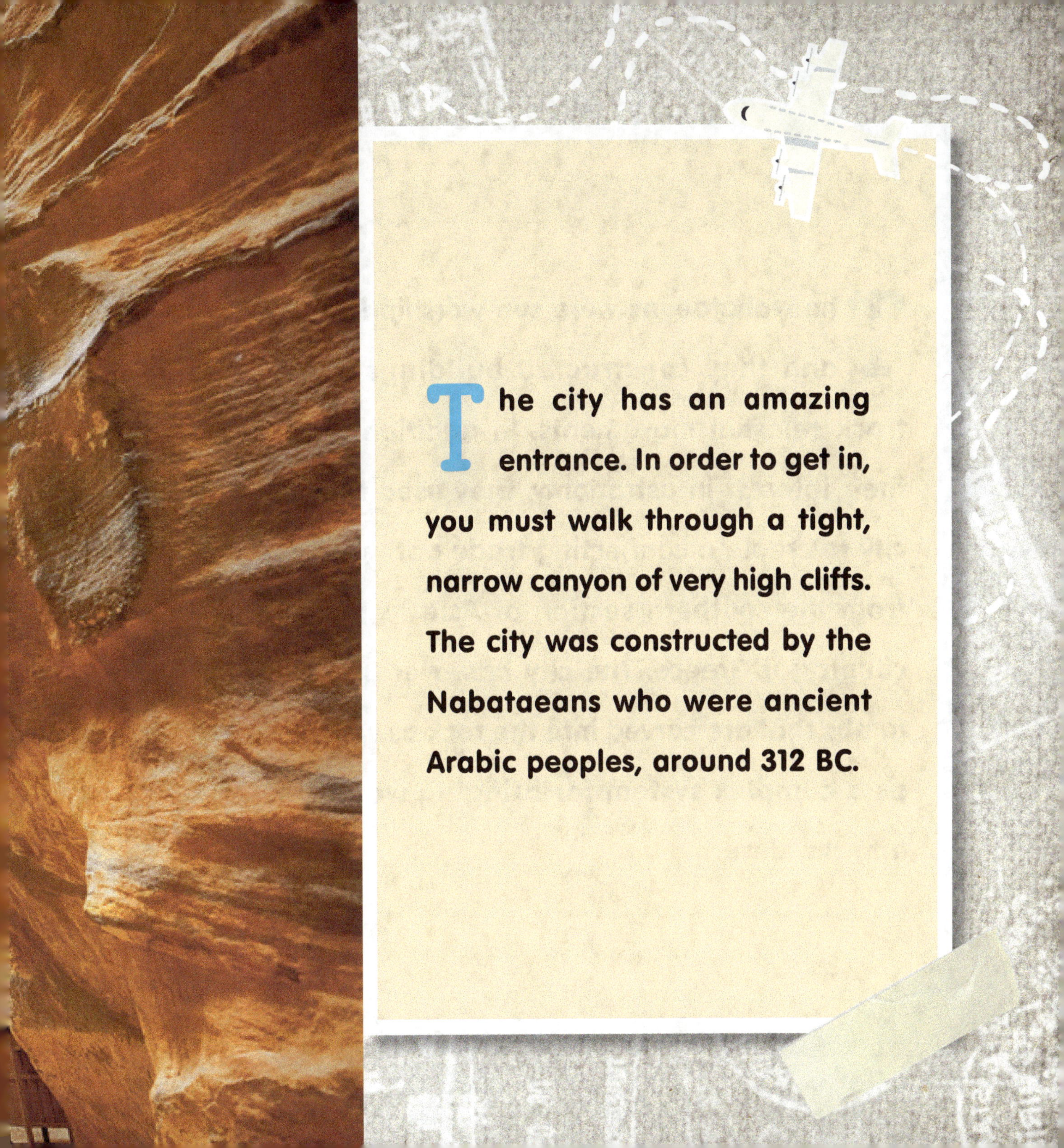

The city has an amazing entrance. In order to get in, you must walk through a tight, narrow canyon of very high cliffs. The city was constructed by the Nabataeans who were ancient Arabic peoples, around 312 BC.

he Nabataeans were sun worshippers and they constructed buildings to track celestial movements. In addition to their interest in astronomy, they used the city to create a connecting trade pathway from the southern section of Asia to the country of Greece. The city has over 800 tombs that are carved into the rock as well as a complex system for bringing water into the desert.

TOMBS

CHRIST THE REDEEMER

One of the most famous landmarks in South America, Christ the Redeemer is an enormous statue of Jesus Christ called Cristo Redentor by the Brazilians. It is about 98 feet in height and towers over the city as it stands on the peak of a mountain called Corcovado, which is over 2,300 feet tall.

The style of the statue is Art Deco, which is a sleek, streamlined design style from the 1920s when the statue was constructed. The designer and construction team began working on the statue in Paris in 1926.

CORCOVADO MOUNTAIN

It was transported from France to Rio de Janeiro, which is the second largest city in Brazil, and was brought up the mountain in segments by railway and assembled on the mountaintop. This amazing

RIO DE JANEIRO

statue welcomes people to Brazil with its open arms.
It was dedicated in 1931 to commemorate Brazil's
independence, which happened in 1831.

The statue stands on a pedestal that is 26 feet in height and houses a chapel where more than one hundred people can worship. The statue is surrounded by a beautiful natural area called the Tijuca Forest, one of the world's largest urban forests with a wide variety of animals and plants.

TIJUCA FOREST

MACHU PICCHU

High in the Andes Mountains of Peru are the mysterious remains of an ancient city known as Machu Picchu. It was built by the Incas and is located close to the site of Cusco, which was the capital city of the once-powerful Incan Empire. The words "Machu Picchu" translate to "old mountain" and they refer to the lower of the two mountain peaks that tower above the city's ruins.

No one lives in the city today and due to its remote location it escaped capture by the Spanish conquistadors when they arrived in Peru in the 16th century. Explorers found the ancient site in the 20th century and marveled at the well-preserved ruins of

temples, farming terraces cut into the steep mountain cliffs, and stone dwellings. The taller mountain peak there, called Huayna Picchu, was home to the Incan priests.

CHICHEN ITZA

Located in the center of the Mexican Yucatán Peninsula, the city of Chichén Itzá was built many centuries ago by the Mayans. Archaeologists don't know the date when the southern section of the city was built, but its northern section was built around the 11th century.

There are quite a few structures remaining in this ancient city, but the most famous is El Castillo. This name was given to it by the Spanish explorers and the words in Spanish mean "the castle."

The structure, which was built about 800 AD, is a step pyramid that was constructed on top of an older structure and built to specifications that relate to the Mayan calendar. Once painted a striking red color and covered in plaster, the pyramid is almost 80 feet in height and was built in honor of the Mayan serpent god, Kukulcan.

At the top of the structure is a temple where Mayan priests offered sacrifices to Kukulcan. Each side of the pyramid has 91 steps, which represent a season. The four groups of 91 steps plus the top platform yield a total of 365 for the days in a year. On the staircase that faces north, there are two sculptures of snakes' heads at the bottom of the stairs.

THE COLOSSEUM

During the 3rd and 5th centuries BC, the Roman Empire was at its peak. Their powerful armies had blazed through Europe, the Middle East, and North Africa, grabbing up territories and cultures as they went. They were violent, especially toward those who stood against them, but they also spread progressive thinking and prosperity across their lands.

At their capital city of Rome, they built an amazing forum with beautiful architecture. Many of these ancient buildings can still be seen today, including the Colosseum, which was a gigantic outdoor amphitheater.

Seats in the front were reserved for the wealthy and powerful and in the back the ordinary people strained their necks to see the entertainment. The entertainment was bloody battles between gladiators

or between a gladiator and a wild beast. There was a
special emperor's box for the emperor and beneath the
Colosseum was the hypogeum where the animals and
equipment were housed prior to and after each event.

THE TAJ MAHAL

The Taj Mahal, which is true to its name meaning "the crown of all palaces," is located in the northern section of India and is known worldwide for its beauty. It was built by Shah Jahan, the emperor of India, in honor of his wife Mumtaz Mahal, whom he dearly loved.

The construction of this perfectly symmetrical structure for their tombs was begun in 1632 and took more than 20 years for 20,000 laborers to complete.

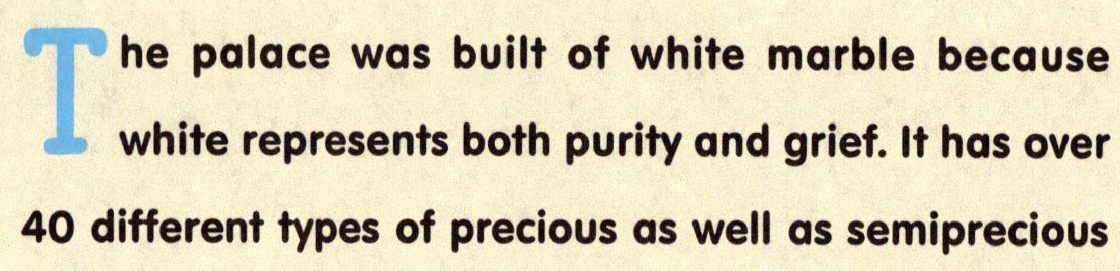

The palace was built of white marble because white represents both purity and grief. It has over 40 different types of precious as well as semiprecious stones and inscriptions from the Islam holy

book, the Qur'an.

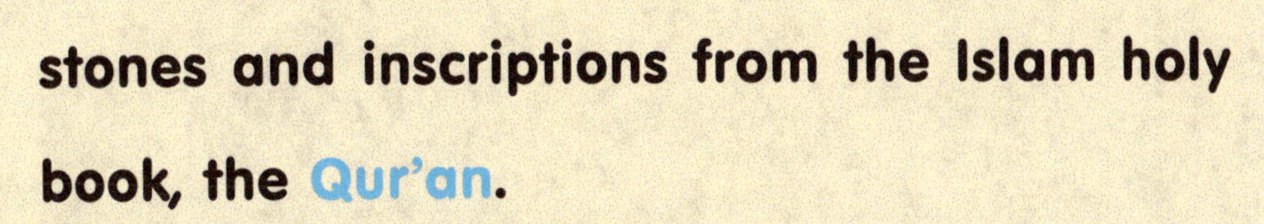

A WORLD OF WONDERS

The seven world wonders are amazing structures built from ancient to modern times. They range from the ancient stone ruins built by the Maya and Inca to the Art Deco statue of Christ the Redeemer built in modern times. As different as they are, they all have one thing in common. They show the range of man's construction ingenuity.

Awesome! Now that you've read about amazing wonders from around the world you may want to read more about the honorary member of the world wonders in the Baby Professor book Exploring the Great Pyramid of Giza: One of the Seven Wonders of the World.

GREAT PYRAMID OF GIZA

Visit

BABY PROFESSOR
EDUCATION KIDS

www.BabyProfessorBooks.com

to download Free Baby Professor eBooks
and view our catalog of new and exciting
Children's Books